SONGS
FOR A
SAVIOR

ADVENT DEVOTIONS

SONGS
FOR A
SAVIOR
ADVENT DEVOTIONS

CONTENTS

FOREWORD

FOREWORD

When a family is preparing for the arrival of a new baby, there is much discussion about what the child's name will be. Out come the baby name books, and everyone has a suggestion. Will it be a boy, or a girl? Will the name be chosen for its meaning? For a time-honored tradition? Will a member of the family, or a treasured friend be commemorated?

As all of heaven prepared for the birth of Jesus, what names did the heavenly hosts think of for God the Son, Messiah?

The first part of this devotional pairs Hannah's Prayer with Zechariah's Prophecy, and the names of the Son of God that come out of their prayers.

HANNAH'S PRAYER

Hannah was the mother of the prophet Samuel, who was the last of the Hebrew Judges and the first prophet to anoint a king of Israel. It was Samuel who anointed King David, recognizing in the young shepherd boy that God does not judge by what the world sees, or by the world's standards, but rather God looks in the heart. The heart and soul are what matter to God for eternity.

ZECHARIAH'S PROPHECY

Zechariah was the father of John the Baptist, who was the last of the Hebrew Prophets, and the Hebrew prophet who heralded and baptized Messiah Jesus, the King of all kings and Lord of all lords. John the Baptist was able to identify the Messiah in the unassuming carpenter and stonemason by God's direct revelation in the form of a dove resting above Jesus's head. Israel was looking for a royal king but God intended to save the world for eternity.

The second part of this devotional pairs Mary's Song with Jesus's Beatitudes, and the names of God the Son which arise.

MARY'S SONG

Mary was the birth mother of Jesus, the first to experience the extraordinary reality of God's very life growing within her. As any mother might do, Mary surely sang lullabies to her baby, and taught Him the scriptures and stories of His people as He grew. It was Mary who heard her Son's first word, and rejoiced over His first step. It is no wonder she "pondered these things in her heart."

JESUS'S SERMON ON THE MOUNT

As His ministry grew, Jesus's teaching became famous, and His Beatitudes continue to engage us thousands of years later with the wonder of the Lord's wisdom.

As you and I meditate on these words, let us think about the names all heaven and earth gave to this tiny, vulnerable baby Who is God the Son. From eternity into our world and then returned to the glory from whence He came, Jesus now opens the way for you and me to be with him in glory forever.

ORDER OF READING

These devotions are divided up according to the traditional Advent season, starting with the first Sunday of Advent four weeks before Christmas. There are two devotions for each Sunday, and one for each following day. In the fourth week of Advent, please flip to the end of the book to read the two devotions for Christmas on whatever day it falls. You can read the remaining devotions in the days following Christmas.

Christ Jesus,

who, though he existed in the form of God,
    did not regard equality with God
    as something to be grasped,

but emptied himself,
    taking the form of a slave,
    assuming human likeness.

And being found in appearance as a human,
    he humbled himself
    and became obedient to the point of death—
    even death on a cross.

Therefore God exalted him even more highly
    and gave him the name
    that is above every other name,

so that at the name given to Jesus
    every knee should bend,
    in heaven and on earth and under the earth,

and every tongue should confess
    that Jesus Christ is Lord,
    to the glory of God the Father.

— Apostle Paul, Philippians 2:5-11

And surely I am with you always, to the very end of the age.

— Jesus, Matthew 28:20 (NIV)

FIRST WEEK
OF ADVENT

Hannah prayed and said,
"My heart exults in the Lord;
  my strength is exalted in my God.
My mouth derides my enemies
  because I rejoice in your victory.
There is no Holy One like the Lord,
  no one besides you;
  there is no Rock like our God.
Talk no more so very proudly;
  let not arrogance come from your mouth,
for the Lord is a God of knowledge,
  and by him actions are weighed.
The bows of the mighty are broken,
  but the feeble gird on strength.
Those who were full have hired themselves out for bread,
  but those who were hungry are fat with spoil.
The barren has borne seven,
  but she who has many children is forlorn.
The Lord kills and brings to life;
  he brings down to Sheol and raises up.
The Lord makes poor and makes rich;
  he brings low; he also exalts.
He raises up the poor from the dust;
  he lifts the needy from the ash heap
to make them sit with princes
  and inherit a seat of honor.
For the pillars of the earth are the Lord's,
  and on them he has set the world.
He will guard the feet of his faithful ones,
  but the wicked will perish in darkness,
  for not by might does one prevail.
The Lord! His adversaries will be shattered;
  the Most High will thunder in heaven.
The Lord will judge the ends of the earth;
  he will give strength to his king
  and exalt the power of his anointed."

— Hannah's Prayer: 1 Samuel 2:1-10

SUNDAY MORNING: HANNAH'S PRAYER

Hannah was the beloved first wife of Elkanah, from the tribe of Ephraim. He was a wealthy landowner, and a devoted husband. However, scripture explains that though Elkanah loved his wife, and though both were godly and devout, the Lord had prevented Hannah from conceiving children.

Elkanah took on a second wife, Peninnah, who was gratifyingly fertile and bore him many children, both sons and daughters. Was it jealousy that prompted Peninnah to drive Hannah to tears, again and again, about her barrenness and Peninnah's bounty?

Finally, one day, Hannah dissolved into tears at the yearly feast in Shiloh, and couldn't eat. Even though her husband spoke compassionately and lovingly to her, she had to excuse herself, and went the Lord's house to pray it all out.

God answered her heartfelt longing with a son, Samuel, the following year. Knowing Samuel was a gift from God, Hannah took him back to the Lord's house after he was weaned, prayed over him, and dedicated him to the Lord to be raised up in God's house by the high priest. Perhaps she was remembering Moses's story, who was raised up in Pharaoh's house by the Egyptian Princess.

Then his father Zechariah was filled with the Holy Spirit and prophesied:

"Blessed be the Lord God of Israel,
for he has looked favorably on his people and redeemed them

He has raised up a mighty savior for us
in the house of his child David,

as he spoke through the mouth of his holy prophets from of old,

that we would be saved from our enemies and from the hand of all who hate us.

Thus he has shown the mercy promised to our ancestors
and has remembered his holy covenant,

the oath that he swore to our ancestor Abraham,
to grant us that we, being rescued from the hands of our enemies,

might serve him without fear, in holiness and righteousness
in his presence all our days.

And you, child, will be called the prophet of the Most High,

for you will go before the Lord to prepare his ways,
to give his people knowledge of salvation
by the forgiveness of their sins.

Because of the tender mercy of our God,
the dawn from on high will break upon us,

to shine upon those who sit in darkness and in the shadow of death,
to guide our feet into the way of peace."

— Zechariah's Prophecy Luke 1:67-79

SUNDAY EVENING: ZECHARIAH'S PROPHECY

Zechariah, and his wife Elizabeth, both from the tribe of Levi and descended from Aaron's high priestly line, also knew what it was to have no children, though they were godly and devout people who would have loved to raise a family. Then Zechariah was visited by the angel Gabriel to tell him the astonishing and glorious news that the aged Elizabeth would now conceive. Zechariah expostulated in disbelief (which earned him the Lord's silencing for the next nine months!).

Perhaps Zechariah began to think about the other couples who had experienced this same favor from God – Abraham and Sarah, Elkinah and Hannah. Because, by the time John was born, Zechariah had fully repented of his disbelief and, carried along by the Spirit, prophesied over his son, recognizing what a miracle he was.

"My heart rejoices in the Lord; in the Lord my horn is lifted high."

— Hannah's Prayer, 1 Samuel 2:1

CHRISTMAS CAROL

The shepherds heard the story

Proclaimed by angels bright,

How Christ, the Lord of glory

Was born on earth this night.

To Bethlehem they sped

And in the manger found Him,

As angel heralds said.

"Lo, How A Rose E'er Blooming"
German carol (15th century)

PRAYER

Almighty God, our hearts rejoice in you, for you have raised up the horn of salvation, you have set us free from oppression and will raise us up on the last day to be with You for all eternity.

"He has raised up a horn of salvation for us in the house of his child David."

— Zechariah's Prophecy, Luke 1:69

MONDAY: ALMIGHTY GOD

THE HORN OF SALVATION

In her jubilation, Hannah employed a well-known symbol of triumph in her day—the call of the shofar proclaiming military victory and release from oppression. Hannah lived during the last generation of the time of the judges, a turbulent era for Israel, when the shofar often blew to communicate a call to arms or give news of battles. She knew it was by the almighty power of God that her prayer was answered.

God also appointed the shofar to announce two important festivals.

The Festival of Trumpets took place on the first day of the seventh month and was to be a time of complete rest.

The Year of Jubilee happened every fiftieth year. On the Day of Atonement, the trumpets would sound to broadcast all debts nullified, all inheritances in the land returned to their original owners, and all those enslaved or serving indentured terms declared free.

Zechariah may have been thinking of these festivals in his prophetic song. In the eternal Jubilee of Messiah, by the almighty power of God, the debts of sin are paid, the prisoners of sin are set free, and our inheritance in the Lord is secured. And when the Lord returns at the shout of archangels, and the sounding of their trumpets, those who find our salvation in Jesus will enter into His rest forever.

CHRISTMAS CAROL

O Savior, Child of Mary,
Who felt our human woe,
O Savior, King of glory,
Who dost our weakness know;
Bring us at length we pray,
To the bright courts of Heaven,
And to the endless day!

"Lo, How A Rose E'er Blooming"
German carol (15th century)

PRAYER

We exalt You, O Lord our Redeemer, for You have reclaimed us from sorrow and woe as the end of our story. We look forward to the bright courts of heaven where You have given us a new destiny.

TUESDAY: REDEEMER

DELIVERANCE

Hannah had patiently endured years of Peninah's public mocking. Even though Hannah was Elkinah's first and most beloved wife, it was Peninah who had been given the position of matriarch in their home, for Peninah had proven a fertile second wife, and provided Elkinah with many heirs. Hannah had born no children at all. Similarly, Zechariah's wife Elizabeth was much loved, but had remained childless.

In that ancient time, a woman's honor came through her children. Even today, there is a deep ache for those who long to have children and have been unable.

Jesus, the Redeemer, also remained unmarried and childless. Though as the oldest brother in His home, He knows what it is to be in a family, and even to raise up children, He still understands the sorrow of not bringing forth a family when one is deeply desired.

God answered Hannah's longing with a son, and several children after her firstborn Samuel. God also brought the joy of a son to Elizabeth and Zechariah. But that is not always God's way. Sometimes, God Who knows and understands our weakness and woe, does not deliver us from our pain, but rather delivers us through our pain. God may sanctify us in this life with long quiet suffering, giving us the hope of eternity to hold in our hearts.

"There is no Holy One like the Lord, no one besides you."

— Hannah's Prayer, 1 Samuel 2:2

CHRISTMAS CAROL

Let all mortal flesh keep silence
And with fear and trembling stand;
Ponder nothing earthly-minded,
For with blessing in his hand
Christ, our God, to earth descending,
Comes our homage to command.

"Let All Mortal Flesh Keep Silence"
Gerald Moultrie (1864)

PRAYER

We bend our knee and our heart before You, Holy One of Israel, for there truly is none like You, holy and humble, mighty God and merciful Messiah. You bring grace and blessing in Your hands, and we offer up our hands to You, to be filled with Your holiness and righteousness.

"That we ... might serve him ... in holiness and righteousness in his presence all our days."

— Zechariah's Prophecy, Luke 1:74-75

WEDNESDAY: HOLY ONE OF ISRAEL

THE HOLY PLACE

Hannah had been so overcome with sorrow and longing she could not eat the feast set before her. Elkinah had given her a double portion, but to Peninah had gone plate after plate loaded with meats and delicacies for her children. On Hannah's side of the table, there was only one place setting. When she could endure Peninah's knowing leers no longer, Hannah quietly slipped away to the tabernacle, and began to pray, so troubled her lips moved, perhaps through quiet sobbing.

Yet in that sacred place the Lord made God's presence known, and Hannah was reassured YHWH of Israel had heard her prayers and would grant her petition.

Zechariah was also in the Holy Place as he ministered to God, bringing before the Lord the incense of the people's prayers while outside the whole assembly of the people were praying aloud. It was then an angel of the Lord appeared to the old priest serving at the altar. Zechariah's unspoken prayers, and those of his wife, would indeed be answered with a son, filled with the Spirit of God.

Both Zechariah and Hannah must have reflected on the gentle yet powerful holiness of God Who is worthy of our grateful homage.

CHRISTMAS CAROL

Sages, leave your contemplations,
Brighter visions beam afar;
Seek the great Desire of nations;
Ye have seen His natal star.

Saints, before the altar bending,
Watching long in hope and fear;
Suddenly the Lord, descending,
In His temple shall appear.

Come and worship, come and worship,
Worship Christ, the newborn King.

"Angels From The Realms Of Glory"
James Montgomery (1816)

PRAYER

Oh Lord, You are our Rock, our refuge, and our foundation stone. Through You we have found life, for You have given us birth, and securely keep us for all eternity.

THURSDAY: ROCK OF HEAVEN

THE ROCK WHO BORE YOU

In her prayer, Hannah spoke of God as a rock, a metaphor first used by Jacob in speaking his prophetic blessing over his son Joseph, saying, "by the name of the Shepherd, the Rock of Israel." Centuries later, Moses spoke of God as the Rock Whose work is perfect, and Whose ways are just, Who is faithful and upright.

"Rock" came to mean the security of a sturdy fortress in which God's people could take confident refuge, and the strength of a seasoned army in which God's people could count on for victory. David, the king Hannah's son would one day anoint, sang of the Lord as his rock, his fortress, and his stronghold.

Moses also spoke of the "Rock Who bore you" and "The God Who gave you birth," and perhaps Hannah had this image in her mind as she prayed and prophesied over her little boy. God had been Hannah's refuge, and through God's mighty power, this precious child had been given birth.

Zechariah envisioned that brighter day when Messiah, the great Desire of all people, would usher in His glorious kingdom. The Rock of Heaven would come to earth to become the cornerstone of faith and the capstone of the Church. Fitted to that Rock would be all the living stones of God's faithful, who would, like Zechariah, be priests who might serve the Lord without fear.

> *"Talk no more so very proudly; let not arrogance come from your mouth."*
>
> — *Hannah's Prayer, 1 Samuel 2:3*

CHRISTMAS CAROL

Frankincense to offer have I;
Incense owns a Deity nigh;
Prayer and praising, voices raising,
Worshiping God on high.

O star of wonder, star of light,
Star with royal beauty bright,
Westward leading, still proceeding,
Guide us to thy perfect light.

"We Three Kings"
John Henry Hopkins Jr. (1857)

PRAYER

Most High God, keep our hearts attuned to You, in praise and thanksgiving, for all we have comes by Your favor. Help us replace arrogance with humility, and to have compassion when fortunes shift.

> *"Blessed be the Lord God of Israel, for he has looked favorably on his people."*
>
> — *Zechariah's Prophecy, Luke 1:70*

FRIDAY: MOST HIGH GOD

HUMILITY IN GOD'S BLESSING

Surely foremost in Hannah's mind were the years of belittling she had endured as Peninah's tents filled with children, and Hannah's trousseau of baby things gathered dust. But her prophetic oracle takes on a much broader application. Life is unpredictable, dramatic change can occur when we least expect it, and in ways we never saw coming. In those moments, we realize afresh how really very little we actually control, that God Most High alone is sovereign over all things.

Hannah's words may also have been for her own complicated feelings. Perhaps she had enjoyed Peninah's discomfiture at Hannah's miraculous, God-given pregnancy, the airing out of her tent to welcome the new little life, and Hannah's position in the heterarchy of their family shifting to the rightful position of matriarch. Hannah may have been sorely tempted to move past enjoyment of God's gifts to gloating over her new-found good fortunes.

Instead, she prayed, do not give arrogance any sway. She had asked for a child, and she now would keep to her vow of leaving him in the care of the Lord and the priest, Eli, and return to a once more empty tent, Samuel's little bed folded up and his things packed away.

Zechariah's prayer brings in the better perspective, to keep our hearts focused on thanksgiving when God grants favor.

CHRISTMAS CAROL

For lo! the days are hastening on,
By prophet seen of old,
When with the ever-circling years
Shall come the time foretold
When peace shall over all the earth
Its ancient splendors fling,
And the whole world send back the song
Which now the angels sing.

"It Came Upon A Midnight Clear"
Edmund H. Sears (1810-1876)

PRAYER

"Search me, O God, and know my heart, try me, and know my thoughts, and see if a grievous way be in me, and lead me in a way age-during" *(Psalm 139:23-24, YLT).*

SATURDAY: WISDOM OF GOD

GOD'S WISDOM LEADS TO COMPASSION

The word Hannah used for "knowledge" is הֵעָדְ | dê'âh, day-aw'; a feminine noun used only six times in the Hebrew scriptures and associated particularly with God. Hannah was surely thinking of God's knowledge of her thoughts and feelings as well as those in her household. Though her husband loved her, he did not seem able to understand or have empathy for her pain. Peninah did not show any interest in friendship with Hannah. Even Eli the priest had accused her of being in her cups, mistaking her distraught and fervent prayer for the mumbling of a drunkard.

God alone knew her heart, and indeed the hearts of all people. As she prayed over her son, Hannah spoke of God's wise understanding which led to God's wise compassion and favor.

This same wise knowledge belongs to Jesus, the One Who "knew all people," Who "knew what was in everyone." Jesus often asked a penetrating question or gave startling insight to the people He met, revealing His divine knowledge of them. For some, this knowledge led to new life. For others, it revealed their settled opposition to God.

Zechariah spoke of God's wise knowledge shared through the prophets, particularly of the birth of Messiah Who would offer God's compassion to all people, One Who would bring healing and peace, but Who would be rejected. One day, this same Messiah will be glorified so that every knee will bow and every tongue confess Him Lord.

SECOND
WEEK
✦OF ADVENT

CHRISTMAS CAROL

Hark! the herald angels sing,
"Glory to the newborn King:
Peace on earth, and mercy mild,
God and sinners reconciled!"
Joyful, all ye nations, rise,
Join the triumph of the skies;
With th'angelic hosts proclaim,
"Christ is born in Bethlehem!"

"Hark! The Herald Angels Sing"
Charles Wesley (1739)

PRAYER

When we are weak You are strong, Omnipotent Lord, and You are trustworthy to use your power for our good and to Your glory. "Amen—the blessing and the glory and the wisdom and the thanksgiving and the honor and the power and the might [be] to our God into the ages of the ages, amen" *(Revelation 7:12).*

"To guide our feet into the way of peace."

— Zechariah's Prophecy, Luke 1:74

SUNDAY MORNING: LORD OMNIPOTENT

THE FULLNESS OF GOD

Both Hannah and Zechariah understood the power of God, for God is the Creator of all that is, seen and unseen. It was by God's omnipotence that both Hannah and Elizabeth found themselves with child. God had done something miraculous that even in that moment was recognized.

Hannah may not have known how important her son would become to the whole arc of Israel's history, that he would become the last Judge of Israel, that he would be a prophet as well as a priest, hearing the very voice of God, and that he would anoint Israel's first two kings. And Elizabeth may not have known how wide a following her son would have, how remarkable his ministry would be, nor how turbulent his life would become.

Yet both Hannah and Elizabeth knew their sons were special because God had moved heaven and earth to bring them into being. Hannah's prophetic oracle would become Mary's Magnificat, and Zechariah's prophetic prayer prepared the way for both to inaugurate the One Whom God would bring forth, God's Own Self in the form of a human being. For the fullness of God is in Jesus, even as a newborn.

CHRISTMAS CAROL

> This Flow'r, whose fragrance tender
> With sweetness fills the air,
> Dispels with glorious splendor
> The darkness everywhere;
> True Man, yet very God,
> From sin and death He saves us,
> And lightens ev'ry load.

"Lo, How A Rose E'er Blooming"
German carol (15th century)

PRAYER

O Lord, Your promised mercy has given us new birth into eternal life. Help us to grow up in every way into Jesus Who is our Head, knit us together as a whole Body, building ourselves up in love, and to enjoy Your blessing *(Ephesians 4:14-16).*

SUNDAY EVENING: HEAD OF THE BODY

MIRACULOUS BIRTH

Perhaps Hannah was thinking of all those feasts where she had but one plate and Peninah had many. Peninah had the full blessings their culture recognized for women—though she was the second wife, she had first position in their home, she was fertile and brought forth many healthy, sturdy children to work their land and be the pride of their father, and the strength of her youth augured a glowing future. Her children would inherit, so she would always have a home.

Hannah's future, on the other hand, grew dimmer with each childless year passing by. For according to the custom of her time, she would likely become a homeless widow one day, prevailing on the kindness of her community for bread and shelter.

But in one masterful stroke, God completely changed the trajectory of Hannah's life. Now it was she who would know a bright future, have a home, and even the promise of grandchildren one day. In the same way, God reverses the fortunes of every repentant sinner who comes to the Lord in faith.

Zechariah also saw the magnificence of God's timing in fulfilling the promise of salvation: the marvelous birth of their son who would come in the spirit of Elijah to proclaim Messiah, and the miraculous birth of Jesus Who in turn would bring forth divine new birth, a Body of whom Christ is the Head.

> *"The barren has borne seven, but she who has many children is forlorn."*
>
> — *Hannah's Prayer, 1 Samuel 2:5*

CHRISTMAS CAROL

What child is this, who, laid to rest
On Mary's lap is sleeping?
Whom angels greet with anthems sweet
While shepherds watch are keeping?
This, this is Christ the King
Whom shepherds guard and angels sing
Haste, haste to bring him laud
The babe, the son of Mary.

"What Child Is This?"
William Chatterton Dix (1865)

PRAYER

In You "all things in heaven and on earth were created, things visible and invisible, whether thrones or dominions or rulers or powers—all things have been created through You and for You" *(Colossians 1:16)*. We praise You for our bodies, for our world, and for divine new birth.

> *"And you, child, will be called the prophet of the Most High."*
>
> — *Zechariah's Prophecy, Luke 1:74*

MONDAY: CREATOR OF ALL THINGS

THE LAST SHALL BE FIRST

Actually, after Samuel, Hannah had three more sons and two daughters, six children in all. It is uncertain how many children Peninah had. Elkinah mentioned ten sons, but he might have been speaking metaphorically. The point, though, is that once Hannah began bearing children, late in life, Peninah's circumstances changed dramatically. When she had been matriarch, Peninah's practice was to provoke Hannah severely, making her life a misery. Now Hannah, once barren, bore both sons and daughters and as first wife displaced Peninah.

But there is a deeper theological truth, here. All throughout the scriptures, God has made it clear the Lord's heart is for the humble and God will lift up the lowly. Those who exalt themselves and make sport of those they deem lesser than will ultimately themselves be brought low by God. As Jesus said, "Whoever wants to be first must be last of all and servant of all (Mark 9:35)."

Being Creator of all things, this is God's to ordain.

When Zechariah turned to his soft and vulnerable baby boy, he spoke of a grand destiny. This son from humble beginnings would become a great prophet. In fact, just as Samuel would be the last Judge of Israel, John would be the last prophet before the Christian era, and both would be known for their humility.

CHRISTMAS CAROL

Glorious now behold him arise;
King and God and sacrifice:
Alleluia, Alleluia,
Sounds through the earth and skies.

O star of wonder, star of light,
Star with royal beauty bright,
Westward leading, still proceeding,
Guide us to thy perfect light.

"We Three Kings"
John Henry Hopkins Jr. (1857)

PRAYER

You are "the beginning, the firstborn from the dead, so that You might come to have first place in everything" *(Colossians 1:18)*. Thank you for being the forerunner, for making a way for us also to arise. We long for the day when we will meet You in the air *(1 Thessalonians 4:16-18)*.

TUESDAY: RESURRECTION AND THE LIFE

NEW LIFE

Some commentators are reluctant to see evidence for the resurrection in the Hebrew scriptures. Yet, Hannah certainly understood the mighty wonder-working power of God to raise us up to life. In a certain way, God had resurrected her own body, making her able to bring forth life. She was like the matriarchs of old, Sarah and Rebekah, and even Rachel, all who received God's miraculous favor in this way. God would do this for Elizabeth a thousand years later.

Jesus demonstrated His power to raise the dead when He said to Martha of Bethany, "I am the resurrection and the life. Those who believe in me, even though they die, will live, and everyone who lives and believes in me will never die. Do you believe this?" She did, and proved it by removing the stone that sealed her brother's tomb (John 11:25-26, 41).

As a first century Jewish priest, Zechariah would have looked forward to the resurrection of the dead and a full restoration of God's original design for creation. Zechariah knew his son would prepare the way for Messiah to establish that Kingdom of Heaven on earth and to bring about the new birth of all those who put their faith in Christ.

CHRISTMAS CAROL

So bring him incense, gold, and myrrh
Come, peasant, king, to own him
The King of kings salvation brings
Let loving hearts enthrone him

This, this is Christ the King
Whom shepherds guard and angels sing
Haste, haste to bring him laud
The babe, the son of Mary.

"What Child Is This?"
William Chatterton Dix (1865)

PRAYER

You are the King of all kings and the Lord of all lords, the whole earth is Yours to command, and the heavens. Every principality whether earthly or heavenly is under Your sovereign reign. Thank You for being a King of peace, of love and grace, and that Your command means life and hope for those who turn to You.

WEDNESDAY: KING OF KINGS

CHRIST IS KING

Hannah wept before the Lord, prayed over her life circumstances, and poured her heart out. She humbled herself under God's hand and in due course God lifted her up. She may not have understood her years of humiliation. But rather than rail against God for her mistreatment, she yielded to God's movement in her life and expressed thanksgiving when God lifted her up. Her prophetic oracle reveals the wisdom, depth of character, and spiritual sensitivity she gained.

Jesus also humbled Himself completely, in the words of an ancient Christian hymn, by emptying Himself, taking on the form of a slave, and becoming obedient even to death on a cross. "Therefore God exalted him even more highly," for Jesus is seated on God's throne, King of kings (Philippians 2:9).

The evidence of God's benevolent, righteous and gracious rule throughout the scriptures provides the ideal governance for humankind, throughout earth's history, in every culture, for every people, in every era. We are indeed thankful that our God is good. Now, as King, Christ commands us to know salvation through Him, and to love one another as He loves us.

CHRISTMAS CAROL

Sinners, wrung with true repentance,
Doomed for guilt to endless pains,
Justice now revokes the sentence,
Mercy calls you; break your chains.

Come and worship, come and worship,
Worship Christ, the newborn King.

"Angels From The Realms Of Glory"
James Montgomery (1816)

PRAYER

O Lord, You have saved a place for each of Your beloved ones at Your banquet table and given us an inheritance of honor in Your Own household. Thank You that Your Covenant of Grace is sealed with the Spirit in each of those who put their faith in You.

THURSDAY: LION OF JUDAH

PROPHETIC UTTERANCE

It is unclear whether all the tribes had begun observing the three feasts God intended to be celebrated together—Sukkot (Feast of Booths), Pesach (Passover), and Shavuot (Pentecost, celebrating the giving of the Torah to Moses). But, as a godly woman married to a Levite, Hannah would have heard the scriptures read at least once a year during the annual festival at Shiloh. It is likely she knew the prophetic blessing Jacob had spoken over his sons and would have understood God's royal intentions for the tribe of Judah.

Decades later, when the now elderly Samuel anointed young David, I wonder if his mother's words came back to him. Samuel knew it was David's heart God saw, the spirit of one who would indeed lift up the poor and needy and would one day literally seat Jonathan's disabled son in a place of honor at David's own table.

Zechariah praised God for remembering this ancient covenant in a fresh way, for now the true Lion of Judah was about to be born. Messiah's eternal reign would not only fulfill and complete God's Covenant of Law, but Jesus would Himself cut a new Covenant of Grace in His own blood.

CHRISTMAS CAROL

Lo, how a Rose e'er blooming

From tender stem hath sprung!

Of Jesse's lineage coming,

As men of old have sung.

It came, a flow'ret bright,

Amid the cold of winter,

When half spent was the night.

"Lo, How A Rose E'er Blooming"
German carol (15th century)

PRAYER

O Lord, You are the One Who is, was, and is to come, You are making all things new, enabling Your Own to triumph. Thank You for the light of hope You give us *(Revelation 1:8, 21:5-7, 22:12-14)*.

FRIDAY: BRIGHT MORNING STAR

PILLARS OF THE EARTH

Hannah acknowledged God's creative power, ordering the laws of the universe, establishing the earth on secure foundations, supporting and upholding the world's existence. Job, whose time preceded Hannah's, also spoke of God's tremendous power, able to "shake the earth out of its place" and to cause even the pillars of the earth to tremble.

Hannah knew God had separated light from darkness, placed the celestial orbs in the heavens and appointed their roles. These lights appeared at different times, and some shone brighter than others. But one light shines the brightest, seen before any other star in the evening and still twinkling every morning when all other stars have winked out: the Morning Star. It is both the first and the last, the Alpha and the Omega of all stars.

Years later, the aged John quoted Jesus in his Revelation saying, "It is I, Jesus ... the Bright Morning Star" (Revelation 22:16).

Zechariah drew from a number of prophecies that spoke of God sending a divine light to dispel darkness, just as dawn breaks over the night sky. The Morning Star was always there, the hope of every generation, and will still be shining when the dawn comes. It is the steady promise of God from the beginning of human history and will be with us for all eternity.

CHRISTMAS CAROL

Joy to the earth, the Savior reigns!
Let all their songs employ,
While fields and floods,
Rocks, hills, and plains,
Repeat, repeat the sounding joy.

"Joy to the World"
Isaac Watts (1719)

PRAYER

Thank You, O God, for so loving the world that You gave to us Your only Son, so that everyone may receive Your gift of salvation through faith. Thank You for Your longsuffering patience, and Your compassionate grace in desiring that none should perish but that all should come to repentance *(John 3:16, 2 Peter 3:9)*.

SATURDAY: SAVIOR

FAITHFUL RESCUE

Hannah lived during a turbulent time in Israel's history. Canaan at the end of the Late Bronze Age and beginning of the early Iron Age was undergoing certain upheavals in changing people groups. The settlement of the Sea Peoples, whom we know as the Philistines, took the coastlands. Israelite tribes lived at a subsistence level in the highlands, while the lowlands supported Canaanite city states. Border skirmishes and highway robbers were common. Often Canaanite warlords, or nearby nations such as Moab, levied heavy tribute requirements. Again and again, when the Israelites cried out to God for rescue, the Lord would raise up a champion to defend them.

Hannah knew from personal experience that God guarded the faithful. And she had lived through times of war when the enemies of God and God's people "perished in darkness".

Something of the same feeling came through in Zechariah's prophecy, for as a first-century Jew Zechariah had seen his fair share of Roman brutality. Yet, he knew the Lord had many times saved God's people from those who hated them—famous stories such as Esther, and later the triumph of the Maccabees, bolstered the people's faith in God's salvation.

The much greater salvation comes in eternity, when God through Christ rescues the faithful from sin, corruption, and death itself.

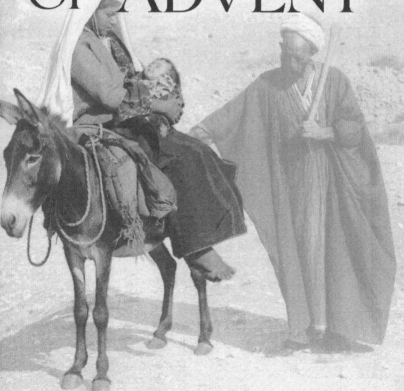

THIRD WEEK
OF ADVENT

And Mary said:

"My soul magnifies the Lord,
*   and my spirit rejoices in God my Savior,*

for he has looked with favor on the lowly state of his
*   servant.*

Surely from now on all generations will call me blessed,
*   for the Mighty One has done great things for me,*
*   and holy is his name;*

indeed, his mercy is for those who fear him
*   from generation to generation.*

He has shown strength with his arm;
*   he has scattered the proud in the imagination of*
*   their hearts.*

He has brought down the powerful from their thrones
*   and lifted up the lowly;*

he has filled the hungry with good things
*   and sent the rich away empty.*

He has come to the aid of his child Israel,
*   in remembrance of his mercy,*

according to the promise he made to our ancestors,
*   to Abraham and to his descendants forever."*

— Mary's Song, Luke 1:46-55

SUNDAY MORNING: MARY'S MAGNIFICAT

Like Hannah and Elizabeth, Mary was godly and devout, full of love for the Lord and wise beyond her years. Unlike Hannah and Elizabeth, Mary was a young girl, betrothed but not yet married.

When Mary was visited by the angel Gabriel to announce the conception of God the Son within her, she wondered in genuine puzzlement how this would come about, as she was a virgin. The angel Gabriel's description of the overshadowing Holy Spirit seemed to make sense to Mary, but it has left the rest of us, over these ensuing millennia, with our jaws dropped.

God's miraculous 'resurrection' of aged bodies, long beyond child-bearing ability, had already rocked centuries of believers. But now God was going to bring something out of nothing, by God's incalculably mighty power—the Lord's Own Person in human form.

Mary understood much of Who this Son would be, and what destiny lay before Him. When she rushed to Elizabeth—the only person who could come close to understanding what was about to happen—she was filled with the Holy Spirit and broke forth in prophetic song.

When Jesus saw the crowds, he went up the mountain, and after he sat down, his disciples came to him.

And he began to speak and taught them, saying:

"Blessed are the poor in spirit, for theirs is the kingdom of heaven.

"Blessed are those who mourn, for they will be comforted.

"Blessed are the meek, for they will inherit the earth.

"Blessed are those who hunger and thirst for righteousness, for they will be filled.

"Blessed are the merciful, for they will receive mercy.

"Blessed are the pure in heart, for they will see God.

"Blessed are the peacemakers, for they will be called children of God.

"Blessed are those who are persecuted for the sake of righteousness, for theirs is the kingdom of heaven.

"... Rejoice and be glad, for your reward is great in heaven."

— Jesus's Beatitudes, Matthew 5:1-10, 12

SUNDAY EVENING: JESUS'S BEATITUDES

Years later, the Lord Jesus Christ echoed the words of his mother Mary in His own teaching. Jesus was raised up in a home which loved and honored God, with parents who took seriously God's command to teach their children all of God's words, even to "talking about them when you sit at home and when you walk along the road, when you lie down and when you get up" (Deuteronomy 11:19).

How often must Mary have sung her Magnificat to her tiny son, as His lullaby? How often did she remind Him of Who His Father truly was, and Who He truly was? Now as a grown man, the Lord fulfilled the destiny His mother had lovingly and faithfully raised Him up in.

CHRISTMAS CAROL

Frankincense to offer have I;
Incense owns a Deity nigh;
Prayer and praising, voices raising,
Worshiping God on high.

O star of wonder, star of light,
Star with royal beauty bright,
Westward leading, still proceeding,
Guide us to thy perfect light.

"We Three Kings"
John Henry Hopkins Jr. (1857)

PRAYER

Thank You, Jesus, for purifying our hearts and for making God known to us. Seeing You we see the Lord *(John 1:18)*.

MONDAY: LORD OF LORDS

MAGNIFICAT

Mary broke into song soon after Elizabeth called her blessed. God could not have been more fully present in that amazing moment. Elizabeth, whose unborn son was already filled with the Holy Spirit, Mary, who carried a child conceived by the overshadowing of Almighty God, and now Elizabeth herself filled with the Spirit as she prophesied over Mary. God in Three Persons literally filled these two mothers, the aging wife of an elderly priest and a young, unmarried girl.

It is no wonder Mary's soul brimmed over with worship, for within her was the unborn Messiah, Jesus, fearfully and wonderfully made, whom God had knit together in secret before even Mary knew He was there. Perhaps Mary spread her hands over her still-flat stomach, knowing in wonderment that within her was the only begotten Son of God the Father. He would be born like any person, yet Jesus alone held within Him the divine glory of God.

Over the ensuing months, Mary would experience Jesus's life growing within her, close to her heart. Once born, Mary would be the most intimately connected with God the Son, first through the throes of labor and birth, then by breast-feeding Him, bathing Him, changing His diapers, teaching Him, guiding Him, comforting Him. Imagine the small and vulnerable Messiah on her lap, falling asleep to the lullaby of her Magnificat.

Mary received Gabriel's message with humble, willing faith in God, and indeed, she was among the first to see God in the flesh.

CHRISTMAS CAROL

Isaiah 'twas foretold it,
The Rose I have in mind;
With Mary we behold it,
The virgin mother kind.
To show God's love aright,
She bore to us a Savior,
When half spent was the night.

"Lo, How A Rose E'er Blooming"
German carol (15th century)

PRAYER

O Lord, Your love is already a great reward here on earth. Help us to say "here am I" with rejoicing when You commission us.

TUESDAY: ANOINTED ONE

HERE AM I

Archangel Gabriel had addressed Mary with the words, "Greetings, favored one!" Already, that tells us a lot about Mary's courage and sense of presence. Mary was favored by God in heaven and blessed among all the women of earth.

Gabriel told her not to fear, because he had come bearing good news: she would bring forth the Son of the Most High God, the promised Messiah, conceived by the Holy Spirit. When she heard it, Mary squared her young shoulders and said, "Here am I, the servant of the Lord; let it be with me according to your word" (Luke 1:38).

There are not that many people in the Bible who said those words to God after receiving a commission. The one who most famously did was Isaiah, in the sanctuary of the temple, before a vision of the Lord, who filled the temple with God's glory. "Then I heard the voice of the Lord saying, 'Whom shall I send, and who will go for us?' And I said, 'Here am I; send me'" (Isaiah 6:8)!

Mary surely understood the implications of being an unwed mother in a culture where that might bring death by stoning. She knew the risk of losing her betrothal, what it might mean to be as a widow, without husband or family homestead, but she also had towering faith in the power, provision, and promise of Almighty God. This was a time to rejoice and sing praise.

CHRISTMAS CAROL

> *And ye, beneath life's crushing load,*
> *Whose forms are bending low,*
> *Who toil along the climbing way*
> *With painful steps and slow,*
> *Look now! for glad and golden hours*
> *Come swiftly on the wing.*
> *O rest beside the weary road,*
> *And hear the angels sing!*

> *"It Came Upon A Midnight Clear"*
> *Edmund H. Sears (1810-1976)*

PRAYER

Lord, thank You for Your promise to hear the desire of the meek, to incline Your ear towards and strengthen the hearts of all who are meek. Thank You that the meek shall obtain fresh joy in You, inheriting the land and delighting in abundance *(Psalm 10:17, 37:11, Isaiah 29:19).*

"Blessed are the meek, for they will inherit the earth."
— *Jesus's Beatitudes, Matthew 5:5*

WEDNESDAY: MEEK AND LOWLY

HUMILITY

In her world, Mary was indeed lowly. Her home in Galilee was disdained by Judeans and her match with a stone-and-wood worker placed her in the lower economic tier. As a Jew, she would have had little standing in Rome-occupied first-century Palestine. And as a woman, Mary had even fewer rights. Perhaps all these things were in her thoughts as she sang of her humble station.

Moreso must have been the scriptures that spoke of God's posture towards the modest and commonplace. Job observed how the Lord lifts up the lowly. The Psalmist spoke of God's regard for the weak and destitute, giving justice and maintaining right for those who had no one else. Most importantly, Proverbs lauded the lowly spirit. Those who choose to serve others receive God's honor.

Years later, Jesus would speak so persuasively about the importance of lowliness, or humility, or meekness that all the apostles echoed the Lord's teaching. The meekness Jesus expressed was not about timidity or enfeeblement, it was about courage and empowerment. It was about patience and generosity of spirit that did not seek first place. Paul described meekness as having the same mind as Christ, looking to the interests of those around us, and in humility regarding others as going before us in importance.

"Surely from now on all generations will call me blessed."
— *Mary's Magnificat, Luke 1:48*

CHRISTMAS CAROL

Hail the heaven-born Prince of Peace!

Hail the Sun of Righteousness!

Light and life to all he brings,

Risen with healing in his wings.

Mild he lays his glory by,

Born that we no more may die,

Born to raise us from the earth,

Born to give us second birth.

"Hark! the Herald Angels Sing"
Charles Wesley (1739)

PRAYER

Thank You, Lord, for blessing us with heavenly peace, and persevering with us throughout life.

"Blessed are the peacemakers, for they will be called children of God."
— *Jesus's Beatitudes, Matthew 5:9*

THURSDAY: PRINCE OF PEACE

DIVINE DELIGHT

The word "blessed" means "divine joy and perfect happiness." There is a steady serenity in this kind of happiness, a supernatural quality that flows from the Holy Spirit deep within. Like love, this joy of blessing can be accessed even during times of trouble and sorrow, for it is the Lord's own life shared with us, God's infinite and eternal blessedness.

Mary understood at least something of the magnitude of what was happening within her. Archangel Gabriel had called her a favored one, whom the Lord was with. Soon after, Elizabeth exclaimed, "Blessed are you among women, and blessed is the fruit of your womb" (Luke 1:42). Years later, during one of Jesus's sermons, a woman called out from the crowd, "Blessed is the womb that bore you and the breasts that nursed you!" Jesus clarified that the true blessing comes from having heard God's word and obeyed it (Luke 11:27-28).

And this was the truth about Mary. She heard God's word, believed in faith, fully yielded herself to God's will, and bore fruit that will last for all eternity.

Jesus would later teach the blessedness of those who being right with God know how to be right with people too. Making peace is active, having courage to walk with others through trouble and sorrow and bring God's truth out, being willing to persevere in love as they deal with the turbulence of their travail, until the process has been completed.

> "Indeed, his mercy is for those who fear him from generation to generation."
>
> — *Mary's Magnificat, Luke 1:50*

CHRISTMAS CAROL

Though an Infant now we view Him,
He shall fill His Father's throne,
Gather all the nations to Him;
Every knee shall then bow down:

Come and worship, come and worship,
Worship Christ, the newborn King.

"Angels From The Realm Of Glory"
James Montgomery (1816)

PRAYER

Thank You, O Lord, for having mercy on us, for Your patience and compassion, for giving us every kindness. Your mercy does bless us, and teaches us to be merciful.

> "Blessed are the merciful, for they will receive mercy."
>
> — *Jesus's Beatitudes, Matthew 5:7*

FRIDAY:
LAMB OF GOD

KINDNESS

Mary knew the Lord's revelation of God's character. It was from one of the more famous passages of her day, and of ours as well. Moses had asked to see God, and God had given a glimpse of the Lord's great glory. God spoke of the Lord's mercy and tenderness, saying, "The Lord, the Lord, a God merciful and gracious, slow to anger, and abounding in steadfast love and faithfulness" (Exodus 34:6). Throughout the scriptures God had proven patient and forbearing, compassionate and forgiving.

God's Law also required the people of God to set themselves apart as a people like their God, to reverence the Lord, and to be generous and merciful as the Lord. Every seven years, the people and the land were to rest as an act of holy benevolence, and every fifty years, all debts were to be forgiven.

In her praise of God, Mary extended the Lord's kindness to all those who would fear God, who would worship the Lord in all humility. All who reverence the Lord belong to God and will receive the Lord's mercy.

Jesus continued to bestow that same kindness throughout His ministry, teaching mercy in all things. Jesus had compassion on the crowds who pursued Him, always ministering to them, restoring those sick, or hurt, or burdened. At the cross, the Lamb of God would offer God's greatest gift of mercy, beginning the work of reconciling all things to Himself (Colossians 1:20).

"He has shown strength with his arm; he has scattered the proud in the imagination of their hearts."

— *Mary's Magnificat, Luke 1:51*

CHRISTMAS CAROL

It came upon the midnight clear,
That glorious song of old,
From angels bending near the earth
To touch their harps of gold:
"Peace on the earth, good will to all,
From heaven's all-gracious King."
The world in solemn stillness lay,
To hear the angels sing.

"It Came Upon A Midnight Clear"
Edmund H. Sears (1810-1876)

PRAYER

Oh how serene and joyful, how deeply satisfied we are when we realize how spiritually impoverished we are without You, and place our whole trust in You, for then You bring us into the Kingdom of Heaven. With the angels, we cry glory, for You are worthy.

"Blessed are the poor in spirit, for theirs is the kingdom of heaven."

— *Jesus's Beatitudes, Matthew 5:3*

SATURDAY: WORTHY

KINGDOM OF HEAVEN

Mary understood the proud, and their own image of themselves. She would have seemed lowly and poor in their estimation. Yet with a sweep of God's Spirit, a humble Galilean would become the mother of God the Son. This was the true reality, the Kingdom of Heaven established on earth, with citizens mighty in spirit, if appearing menial and commonplace to the proud.

The Kingdom of Heaven is now within every person who has placed their faith in Jesus, and in whom God abides. Christ is recognized as king in this realm, for He is worthy of honor as well as of love. The angels have always existed in this Kingdom, that is why they cry "Holy" and glorify God.

Imagine how quiet everyone must have gotten when Jesus said, "Oh how delighted and joyful are people whose spirits are in abject poverty, who are beaten to their knees in spiritual destitution, so desperate they are beyond downtrodden and oppressed." How could that be? Because they are poor enough to qualify as citizens of the Kingdom of Heaven. They know they have no earthly resources whatsoever. They are so humbled and helpless that they put their whole trust in God.

FOURTH
WEEK
OF ADVENT

CHRISTMAS CAROL

No more let sins and sorrows grow
Nor thorns infest the ground;
He comes to make his blessings flow
Far as, far as the curse is found.

"Joy to the World"
Isaac Watts (1719)

PRAYER

Lord, we thank You for the cleansing flow of Your forgiveness whenever we come to You in confession, and for giving us fresh draughts of Your living water, that Your Spirit may well up in us a fountain of life *(John 4:10, 1 John 1:9)*.

SUNDAY MORNING: LIVING WATER

THE RIVER DAN

"Living water" means "moving water," clean water rippling through brooks and fountains, and rivers. Not far from where Hannah lived, the sparkling blue Dan River bubbles up and tumbles out, one of the most beautiful sights in all Israel. It is the largest of the Jordan River's three tributaries, and flows from the melted snow on Mount Hermon. Like the strength of a cascading river, Hannah could say with confidence, "not by might," but by persevering faith. It was surely not the first time Hannah prayed for God's favor. But when it was time, Eli gave Hannah the word from God she was longing for, a word that would reassure her she was noticed, she mattered, and she would receive the blessing that had long been barred to her.

Every year Hannah heard of God's blessing and favor through the parted Red Sea, water that flowed from rocks in the wilderness at God's command, the Jordan which parted as Israel passed into the Promised Land. Every year God caused the flow of rain from the sky, streams to ripple in their hilly, rocky land, and underground springs to feed their wells. Mightier than a conquering army, God's blessing of fresh water enabled the Israelites to prevail.

Zechariah's prophecy of salvation foreshadowed Jesus's proclamation on the temple steps, "Let anyone who believes in me drink ... out of the believer's heart shall flow rivers of living water" (John 7:37-38).

> *"He has filled the hungry with good things and sent the rich away empty."*
>
> — *Mary's Magnificat, Luke 1:53*

CHRISTMAS CAROL

King of kings, yet born of Mary,
As of old on earth he stood,
Lord of lords in human likeness,
In the body and the blood
He will give to all the faithful
His own self for heav'nly food.

"Let All Mortal Flesh Keep Silence"
Gerard Moultrie (1864)

PRAYER

Thank You, O Lord, for preparing a banquet of righteousness for those who come to you longing to be filled.

> *"Blessed are those who hunger and thirst for righteousness, for they will be filled."*
>
> — *Jesus's Beatitudes, Matthew 5:6*

SUNDAY EVENING: BREAD OF LIFE

FEAST FOR THE FAMISHED

Mary's prophetic word was later repeated by Jesus in a slightly different context. Messiah was dining with tax collectors and other "sinners," which caught the notice of a number of Pharisees. They questioned Jesus, surely in consideration of "guilt by association," of concern that Jesus's presence might in some way be indicating Jesus—or even God—condoned the life choices of the people He was publicly befriending. Jesus replied, "Those who are well have no need of a physician, but those who are sick. Go and learn what this means, 'I desire mercy, not sacrifice.' For I have not come to call the righteous but sinners." Jesus's meaning was clear (Mark 2:17).

Mary's meaning is also clear. Those who consider themselves well-fed are not interested in more food. Only those who come hungry will be fed, for it is only they who will eat.

Jesus spoke of a particular kind of hunger, a longing for true righteousness, to have God's character, hold God's values, and live out God's way before the Lord and with others. When you and I receive Christ's Spirit, then we are filled with all that can satisfy our spiritual hunger.

"Oh how serene and joyful, how filled with God's goodness is the person who longs for righteousness in the way a famished person longs for food and a parched person longs for drink, because that person will be truly satisfied."

59

CHRISTMAS CAROL

Christ, by highest heaven adored,
Christ, the everlasting Lord,
Late in time behold him come,
Offspring of the Virgin's womb:
Veiled in flesh the Godhead see;
Hail th'incarnate Deity,
Pleased with us in flesh to dwell,
Jesus, our Immanuel.

"Hark! The Herald Angels Sing"
Charles Wesley (1739)

PRAYER

O Lord, how thankful we are that You, compassionate and just Lord, will judge. Strengthen our inner being with the power of Your Spirit that Christ will dwell in our hearts through faith. Ground us in love, fill us with Your fullness *(Ephesians 3:14-19)*.

"That we would be saved from our enemies."

— *Zechariah's Prophecy, Luke 1:71*

MONDAY: ETERNAL JUDGE OF THE LIVING AND DEAD

COMPASSIONATE AND JUST

Moved by the Holy Spirit and speaking from God, Hannah affirmed God's sovereignty over all people and the arc of God's plan for eternity. It was a bold saying, for in her day every nation had their own pantheon of gods, and it was understood each people group answered to their own deity. But those who belonged to YHWH understood the Lord is far above all over gods, and all the peoples of earth belong to God.

Hannah's oracle moved beyond the first coming of Christ to Messiah's Second Advent, when Jesus comes in glory to judge the living and the dead. God intends to spread justice to all people, making right all that has been wrong, to release the cosmos from its chains to corruption and death, to cleanse all creation from evil.

Other ancient gods—Ba'al, Chemosh, Astarte, the gods of Egypt—were capricious beings without real sympathy for their subjects. But YHWH came to all people as a human being, and is now able to "sympathize with our weaknesses … who in every respect has been tested as we are, yet without sin" (Hebrews 4:15). This is Who will judge all people, One Who knows us deeply, understands us completely, Who loves us without measure, and longs that every person may come to repentance.

This is the loving God Hannah knew and Zechariah trusted in to rescue them.

"He has come to the aid of his child Israel, in remembrance of his mercy."

— *Mary's Magnificat, Luke 1:54*

CHRISTMAS CAROL

Why lies He in such mean estate,
Where ox and ass are feeding?
Good Christian, fear: for sinners here
The silent Word is pleading.

This, this is Christ, the King,
Whom shepherds guard and angels sing:
Haste, haste to bring Him laud,
The Babe, the Son of Mary!

"What Child Is This?"
William Chatterton Dix (1865)

PRAYER

O Lord, so often we come to you weary, with our hearts heavy-laden. We carry weighty burdens, in desperate need of the rest You promise, and to learn from You, for You are gentle and humble in heart. In You we will find rest for our souls *(Matthew 11:28-29).*

"Blessed are those who mourn, for they will be comforted."

— *Jesus's Beatitudes, Matthew 5:4*

TUESDAY: COMFORTER

COMFORT FOR HEARTACHE

God often reminded the people of Israel that the Lord kept covenant with them for the sake of God's past promises of mercy. It is to this heavenly compassion God's people would appeal, such as when the Psalmist prayed, "Redeem us for the sake of your steadfast love" (Psalm 44:26).

Now Mary pronounced the fulfillment of God's gracious benevolence. She spoke of Israel as a child even as she rejoiced in the child she held within her and would soon hold in her arms, close to her heart.

Years later, Jesus spoke of God's mercy and compassion in the imagery of comfort through sorrow. He used the strongest word possible for mourning, a passionate lament of heart-wrenching grief and anguish over indescribable loss, or terrible transgression. With aching heart and flowing tears, the more you and I hurt, the more we might be willing to receive the compassion and comfort of God.

God's consolation brings a deep satisfaction and awareness of being seen, known, and loved, or forgiven. God's reassurance refreshes and restores, filling heavy hearts with hope: "Oh how serene and joyful, how deeply comforted is the person who is desperately sad, or desperately sorry, whose heart is broken, because God has profound comfort for that person."

CHRISTMAS CAROL

Joy to the world, the Lord is come
Let Earth receive her King
Let every heart prepare Him room
And Heaven, and Heaven, and nature sing!

"Joy to the World"
Isaac Watts (1719)

PRAYER

Lord, You are indeed Mighty God, the Most High God, Who commands the heavens and rules the earth. Your promises are trustworthy and Your faithfulness is forever. Keep our hearts steadfast in the confidence that You will indeed rescue Your people.

WEDNESDAY: DELIVERER

GOD'S PRESENCE

As Hannah drew to the close of her oracle, a vision of God filled her eyes. Perhaps she was remembering the stories of Exodus, of YHWH overpowering all the formidable gods of Egypt by hurling thunder, hail, and fire down from heaven. When the people gathered in the wilderness to covenant with YHWH, Mount Sinai shook with the thunder of God's presence in cloud and fire. Later, Hannah's son Samuel would hear the thunder of God's voice as he offered up burnt sacrifices in preparation for battle, and when he called upon the Lord to send a thunderstorm of rain to the thirsty ground.

But Hannah was delivering a much farther-reaching prophecy, prefiguring the Day of the Lord, when all would behold God and Christ, seated upon the throne from which will come mighty thunderpeals and flashes of lightning. Centuries after Hannah's prayer, Isaiah and Ezekiel would also prophecy of God's Presence and Advent in thunder, earthquake, whirlwind, and flame.

Such a mighty Lord is able to rescue God's people from the hands of their enemies, as Zechariah testified. God would uphold God's oath for all eternity to the children of Abraham, who rejoiced when he envisioned Jesus's day. Later, Paul explained that all who share in Abraham's faith are his children and receive his inheritance in God's promises and covenants.

CHRISTMAS CAROL

He rules the world with truth and grace
And makes the nations prove
The glories of his righteousness
And wonders, wonders of his love.

"Joy to the World"
Isaac Watts (1719)

PRAYER

Thank You, Lord, for meekly enduring abuse and suffering for our sake. Just as you entrusted Yourself to the One Who judges justly, so we entrust ourselves to You Who are faithful and true. In You we died to all that is unrighteous, and have been raised to live for righteousness *(1 Peter 2:22-23).*

"Blessed are those who are persecuted for the sake of righteousness, for theirs is the kingdom of heaven."

— Jesus's Beatitudes, Matthew 5:10

THURSDAY: FAITHFUL AND TRUE

PERSECUTION

Mary was among the many who had little agency in their world. Even when they obeyed every authority, paid all the taxes asked of them (which included steep side fees, payable to the tax collector's private account), and did their best to keep clear of political or religious controversy, they were the lowly. Those in power were often capricious or cruel. Their only hope for deliverance was in the Lord.

Mary knew her firstborn was the key to God's liberation. One day, Messiah would bring down those who oppressed and abused the lowly, and He would lift up all those downtrodden and weighed low with burdens.

Jesus, Faithful and True, will come in power to establish righteousness and justice throughout the cosmos. But before this, Jesus came in meekness, His power held in check, suffering persecution as one of the lowly. It was the only way to bring down the most powerful of evil, sitting upon its throne of sin, corruption, and death.

Citizens of the Kingdom of Heaven are not surprised when the forces of darkness oppose the light and life of the Gospel. All those who are persecuted for doing what is right, for being meek or merciful, for offering forgiveness, or restoration, or reconciliation, are sharing in this life of Christ.

"The Lord will judge the ends of the earth; he will give strength to his king and exalt the power of his anointed."

— Hannah's Prayer, 1 Samuel 2:10

CHRISTMAS CAROL

Rank on rank the host of heaven
Spreads its vanguard on the way
As the Light from Light, descending
From the realms of endless day,
Comes the pow'rs of hell to vanquish
As the darkness clears away.

"Let All Mortal Flesh Keep Silence"
Gerard Moultrie (1864)

PRAYER

You are the Light of the World, the Life that is the Light of all people. Your Light shines in darkness and the darkness cannot grasp You, nor overcome You. Thank You for filling those who have put their faith in You with Your Life and Your Light *(John 1:4-5)*.

"To shine upon those who sit in darkness and in the shadow of death."

— Zechariah's Prophecy, Luke 1:79

FRIDAY: LIGHT OF THE WORLD

SHEKINAH

Hannah's Israel was a consortium of tribes who collaborated in times of war and were led by Levi's tribe in worshipping YHWH together at Shiloh. They had periodic champions called judges but were unique among the surrounding peoples in having no king but God. Judge Gideon, perhaps a hundred years earlier, had even said, "I will not rule over you … the Lord will rule over you" (Judges 8:23).

Yet Hannah envisioned the Lord strengthening God's king and empowering God's anointed. Though her son would one day anoint kings at God's behest, the Anointed she beheld was surely Messiah, the One to come, prophesied by Moses.

And though Zechariah was praying over his own son, he was also speaking of One even greater, Whose transcendent light would illuminate even the darkest shadow of death. This is the light of God's glory, Shekinah, the pillar of cloud and fire Who had protected and guided them, Who dwelt among them in the tabernacle, and later the temple.

Three of Jesus's disciples literally beheld Jesus as the Light of the World when He was transfigured before their eyes, God's glory emanating from within Jesus's body. Paul later wrote of the light of the Gospel shining into our own hearts.

"... according to the promise he made to our ancestors, to Abraham and to his descendants forever."

— *Mary's Magnificat, Luke 1:52*

CHRISTMAS CAROL

At his feet the six-winged seraph,
Cherubim with sleepless eye,
Veil their faces to the presence
As with ceaseless voice they cry:
"Alleluia, alleluia!
Alleluia, Lord Most High!"

"Let All Mortal Flesh Keep Silence"
Gerard Moultrie (1864)

PRAYER

How grateful we are, O Lord, that You are present in every place, even in the darkest valley, or the loneliest wilderness, or in the slough of despond. You are with us and for us forever.

"And remember, I am with you always, to the end of the age."

— *Jesus's Great Commission, Matthew 28:20*

SATURDAY: FINISHER OF FAITH

FAITHFUL FOREVER

One of the distinctives of Judaism is this tracing back to a single progenitor of faith and fatherhood, for Abraham is both the predecessor of a people and the pioneer of monotheism. In the conclusion to her magnificent praise to Mighty God, Mary called upon the first promise the Lord made to Abraham. "I will make of you a great nation, and I will bless you and make your name great, so that you will be a blessing," God had promised this founding patriarch. "I will bless those who bless you, and the one who curses you I will curse." God would surround the people descended from Abraham with protection and care (Genesis 12:1-2).

But the promise Mary indicated came at the end of God's prophetic consecration: "and in you all the families of the earth shall be blessed." It was a promise millennia old, and would extend into eternity (Genesis 12:3).

Jesus returned to this promise in His instructions to His closest followers and students. They were to be the instrument of Jesus's blessing, the promised blessing of God. Matthew remembered Jesus telling them to make disciples of those from every kind of background, to baptize them into the faith, and to teach them to live by everything Jesus had taught. John remembered Jesus saying to feed and tend His lambs.

By His Spirit, Jesus is now with us, and will be with us forever.

CHRISTMAS

CHRISTMAS CAROL

God from true God, and
Light from Light eternal,
Born of a virgin, to earth he comes!
Only-begotten Son of God the Father:

O come, let us adore him,
Christ the Lord!

"O Come, All Ye Faithful"
John Francis Wade (1841)

PRAYER

Lord, You are the Mighty One, Whose creative power brought forth the universe as we know it, something out of nothing. Yet the wonderful mystery of Your infinite and eternal Being becoming the only-begotten Son of God overwhelms us with awe. To You belongs all glory, honor, wisdom, power, and praise.

The virgin will conceive and give birth to a son.
— *Matthew's Testimony, Matthew 1:23*

CHRISTMAS MORNING: ONLY BEGOTTEN

A TRUE VIRGIN

Perhaps Mary and Elizabeth sat together at some point and remembered all the women throughout the scriptures in whom God had miraculously quickened life. There were, of course, the matriarchs Sarah, Rebekah, and Rachel. There was also Manoah's wife, the mother of Samson, Hannah, a woman from Shunem, and now Mary and Elizabeth. Each account gave testimony to the supernatural strength of the Lord.

But Mary's narrative alone bore witness to the wonder-working creative power of God to bring forth something out of nothing, for the Spirt of God would overshadow Mary and within her would form the unique Son of God.

But would people understand this mystery?

Matthew's testimony is careful to explain it. The apostle first quoted the prophet Isaiah's oracle, "Look, the virgin shall become pregnant and give birth to a son." In the original Hebrew, Isaiah had used a word that meant "young woman," meaning usually unmarried and presumably a virgin. However, הָעַלְמָה |'almâ could also refer to a newly married young woman.

But in the Septuagint, the 2,300-year-old Greek translation of the Hebrew scriptures, the ancient translators chose the word παρθένος | parthenos, which only means "virgin." Matthew quoted from the Septuagint.

"And," Matthew continued, "Joseph had no marital relations with her until she had given birth to a son" (Matthew 1:25).

"And holy is his name."

— Mary's Magnificat, Luke 1:49

CHRISTMAS CAROL

Yea, Lord, we greet thee,

born this happy morning;

Jesus, to thee be all glory giv'n!

Word of the Father, now in flesh appearing:

O come, let us adore him,

Christ the Lord!

"O Come, All Ye Faithful"
John Francis Wade (1841)

PRAYER

You are God with us, God and human, the One Who champions us against all the forces of darkness and evil. All of scripture, from first to last, is about You. You are the Alpha and Omega of human history.

And they will call him Immanuel (which means "God with us").

— Matthew's Testimony, Matthew 1:23

CHRISTMAS EVENING: ALPHA AND OMEGA

GOD WITH US

Giving birth involves great effort. It is an earthy as well as an earthly labor, with suffering and strenuous toil, drawing all the mother has within her to bring forth this small and vulnerable life. Afterwards, she is spent, exhausted from the work of growing and birthing a new human being. Imagine, then, the trembling and drained young virgin holding her newborn son. In her heart, she rejoices in his healthy cry, in the strength of his pull as he drinks in her milk.

Perhaps she sheds soft tears of thanksgiving. Through her the protevangelium had been fulfilled this night, the first gospel oracle, spoken in God's own voice, "the seed of the woman" who would one day have victory over evil itself.

This is a sacred moment, one held in hush, for Messiah is here, God is with us. Before the heavens spread open with all the angelic host singing hallelujah, there is this quiet tableau. "Your name is holy," Mary must have whispered. "Your name is Immanuel," Joseph would have whispered.

Matthew's testimony captures something of this sense, for the Lord was with God's people in the most intimate way yet, as a person, fully God and fully human. The Word of God made flesh was how John's testimony began, a mystical mystery so incomprehensible that it still takes our breath away. And the writer of Hebrews says this God/Man is like us in every way.

Joanne Guarnieri Hagemeyer led and taught a Bible class of 350-500 students from 2003 to 2013, then retired in 2018 as an advisor and mentor to sixteen Bible classes in the Maryland area with BSF, International. She now writes for Grace and Peace Joanne, LLC, and serves on the pastoral and teaching team of New Hope Chapel, Arnold, MD.

A long-time "armchair archaeologist," she joined the Board of Directors of the Biblical Archaeology Forum in 2013 and now serves as Vice President. she has participated in two excavations, Tel Kabri and Tel Akko, and is now part of the Akko Study Team. Joanne also serve as a lay counselor and trainer in affiliation with The Lay Counselor Institute.

After earning her Masters in Theological Studies, Joanne is continuing her education at Portland Seminary in the Doctor of Ministry, Semiotics program.

More of Joanne's writing and video content can be found on her website, graceandpeacejoanne.com.

Made in the USA
Columbia, SC
26 November 2024

47495764R00052